Make Your Own Art

Origami

Sally Henry and Trevor Cook

PowerKiDS
press.

New York

Published in 2011 by The Rosen Publishing Group, Inc.
29 East 21st Street, New York, NY 10010

Text and design: Sally Henry and Trevor Cook
Editor: Joe Harris
U.S. editor: Kara Murray
Photography: Sally Henry and Trevor Cook

Library of Congress Cataloging-in-Publication Data

Henry, Sally.
 Origami / by Sally Henry and Trevor Cook.
    p. cm. — (Make your own art)
 Includes index.
 ISBN 978-1-4488-1586-9 (library binding) — ISBN 978-1-4488-1619-4 (pbk.) —
ISBN 978-1-4488-1620-0 (6-pack)
1. Origami—Juvenile literature. I. Cook, Trevor, 1948- II. Title.
 TT870.H426 2011
 736'.982—dc22
                        2010025458

Printed in the United States

SL001624US

CPSIA Compliance Information: Batch #WA11PK: For Further Information contact Rosen Publishing, New York, New York at 1-800-237-9932

Contents

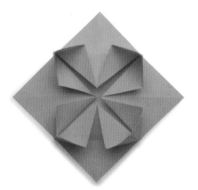

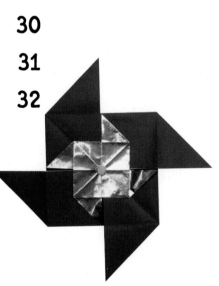

Introduction

The folk art of origami has been popular in Japan for hundreds of years. Now it is an art form loved around the world.

The idea is to make a work of art by folding just one sheet of paper. All you need is a clean, clear work space, clean hands and some paper!

Japanese origami paper squares

Paper

Origami paper needs to be strong so it can be folded and refolded many times without tearing. It shouldn't be too thick, as that would make folding many layers hard. Origami paper is usually square and colored on one side. It generally measures between 6 and 8 inches (150–200 mm) square.

Folds

Nearly all projects in origami have just a few kinds of folds. Learn the names of these and it will make the instructions easier to follow later on. We use symbols to explain what happens between the pictures. Learn what they mean as we go along.

Symbols

valley fold	– – – – – – –
mountain fold	–·–·–·–·–
hidden fold	··················
existing crease	————
divide into equal parts	⊢⊢⊢⊢
direction to move paper	↗
fold point to point	⤷
turn the paper over	↻
turn the paper around	↻ 90°
push	◄

Valley, mountain, and book folds

1

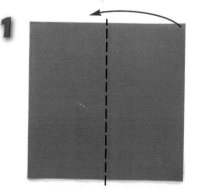

Here's a piece of origami paper. Fold it down the middle like this. We call this a **valley fold**.

2

The mark left by folding is called a crease.

Folding a square of paper in this way is called a **book fold**, because it makes a book shape.

3

If you fold the paper away from you instead, you get a **mountain fold**.

4

Cupboard fold

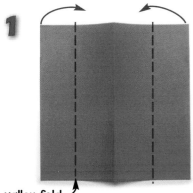

1

valley fold

Make a mountain fold down the middle of the paper.

2

Fold the sides to the middle, using the center crease as a guide. This is a **cupboard fold**.

3

equally spaced creases

Open the sides right out and you can see that we've divided the square into four equal parts.

Diagonal fold

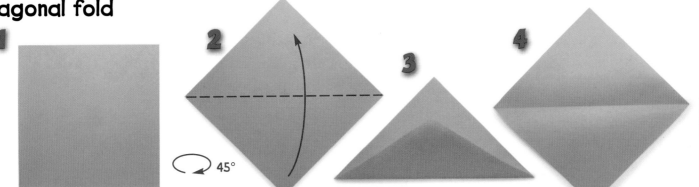

1

2

45°

3

4

5

Turn your paper through 45 degrees to make the **diagonal fold**.

Inside reverse fold

1 Start with a diagonal-folded corner. Make a new valley fold across the end to make a crease.

2 Open the corner and change the new valley fold on the upper side into a mountain fold, and the mountain fold into a valley.

3 Gently ease the folded tip back inside as you close the main fold.

4 Finish by pressing down firmly.

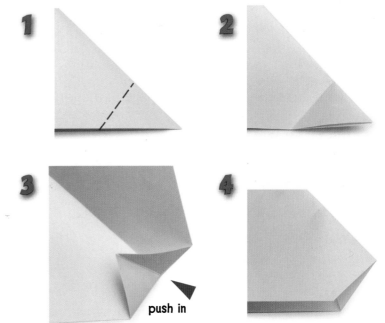

1

2

3

push in

4

inside reverse fold

Outside reverse fold

1 Beginning with another diagonal-folded corner, mountain fold the end to make a crease.

2 Open the corner and convert the new mountain fold on the upper side to a valley fold and the existing mountain fold to a valley fold.

3 Ease the folded tip back over the corner, at the same time closing the main fold.

4 Press down to establish the new fold.

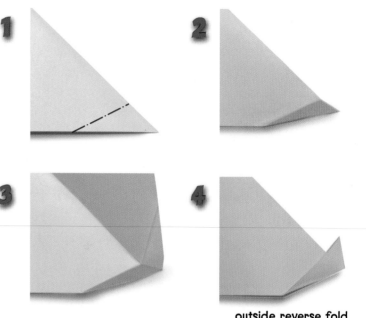

outside reverse fold

Bases

Many origami designs share the same early stages. They are often named after the most common designs to which they lead. Here are some common ones that will appear later in this book.

Kite base

1 Fold one side into the middle.

2 Repeat with this side.

3 kite base

Start with a diagonal crease (see page 5, diagonal fold, picture 3).

Square base

1 valley fold

2 valley fold / mountain fold

3 Rotate the paper 45° and push the sides in and the top down.

4 square base

Make two diagonal creases, then turn the sheet over and make two book creases.

Water bomb base

The same method that makes the square base can be used to produce the water bomb base. Fold the square like the square base, but reverse the folds.

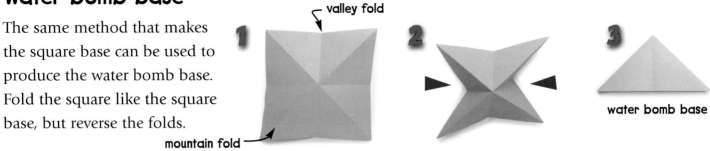

valley fold

mountain fold

1

2

3 water bomb base

Bird base

The bird base is named after the many bird designs that begin with it. Start with a square base.

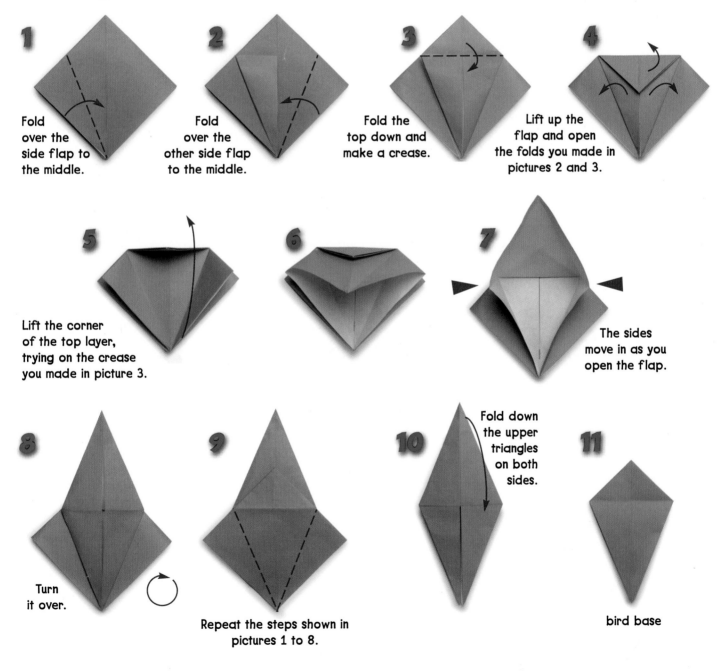

1 Fold over the side flap to the middle.

2 Fold over the other side flap to the middle.

3 Fold the top down and make a crease.

4 Lift up the flap and open the folds you made in pictures 2 and 3.

5 Lift the corner of the top layer, trying on the crease you made in picture 3.

6

7 The sides move in as you open the flap.

8 Turn it over.

9 Repeat the steps shown in pictures 1 to 8.

10 Fold down the upper triangles on both sides.

11 bird base

Garden Bird

Brighten up your garden with this colorful bird!

10 MINUTES

Start with a kite base (see page 6).

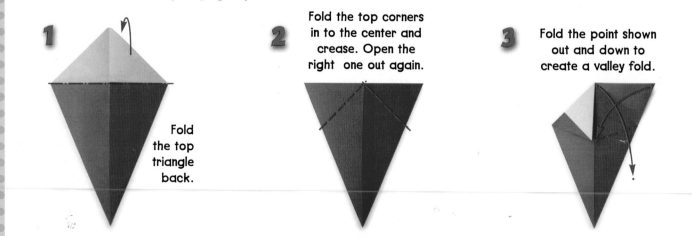

1 Fold the top triangle back.

2 Fold the top corners in to the center and crease. Open the right one out again.

3 Fold the point shown out and down to create a valley fold.

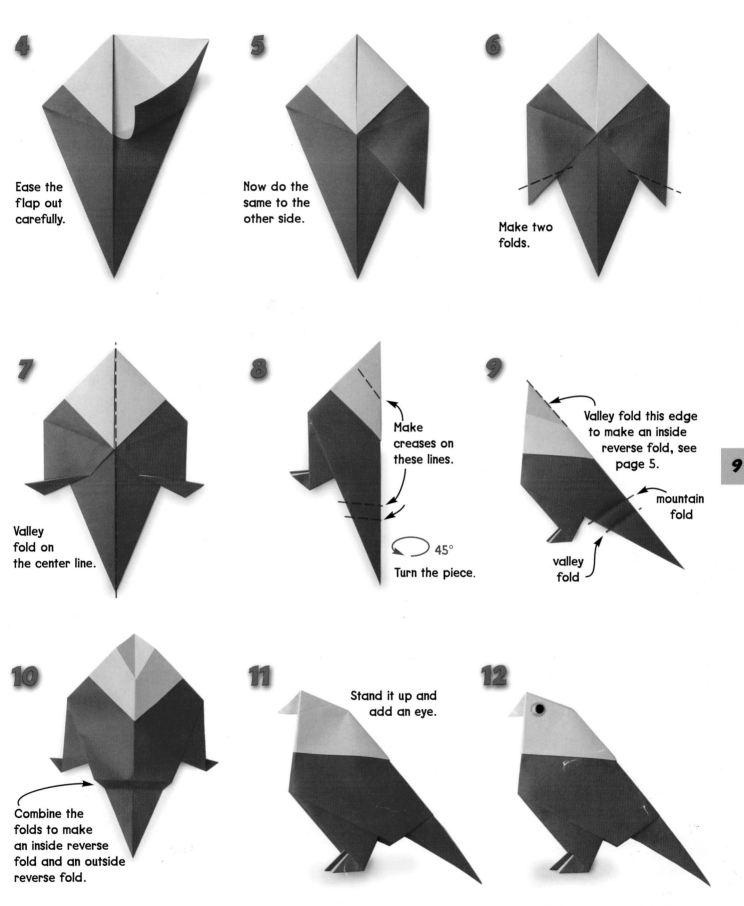

4 Ease the flap out carefully.

5 Now do the same to the other side.

6 Make two folds.

7 Valley fold on the center line.

8 Make creases on these lines.

↺ 45°

Turn the piece.

9 Valley fold this edge to make an inside reverse fold, see page 5.

mountain fold

valley fold

10 Combine the folds to make an inside reverse fold and an outside reverse fold.

11 Stand it up and add an eye.

12 And there's your bird!

Lotus Flower

This flower makes a pretty table decoration!

Let's start with two diagonal folds (see square base, page 6, picture 2).

1 Fold the corners to the middle.

2 Turn the paper over.

3 Cupboard fold the top and bottom (see page 5).

4

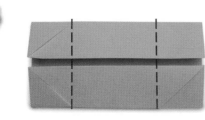

Cupboard fold the sides.

5

Turn over.

6

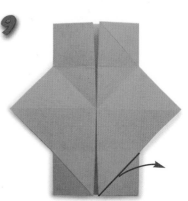

Open the four corners from the middle.

7

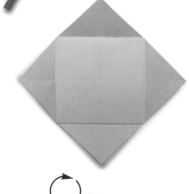

Turn over.

8

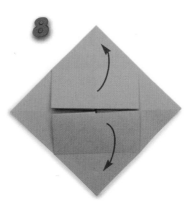

Open the doors.

9

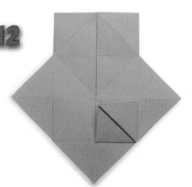

Lift this edge and move it to the right.

10

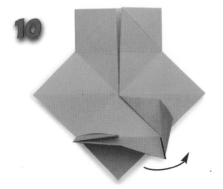

Refold the flap . . .

11

. . . into the new position.

12

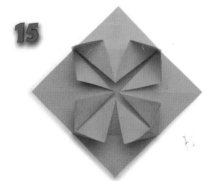

It should now look like this.

13

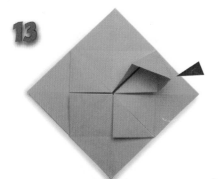

Repeat the moves in the steps from 9 to 12 to make the other three petals.

14

Open the four petals.

15

Here's the completed flower!

Jumping Frog

Fold a pair of frogs and have a jumping contest!

20 MINUTES

12

We're going to make two frogs from one paper square.

1 Cut the square exactly in two, then fold one of the pieces in half.

2

Fold the top corners to the middle.

3

Open the folds, then fold the top down.

4

Fold the corners to the middle again.

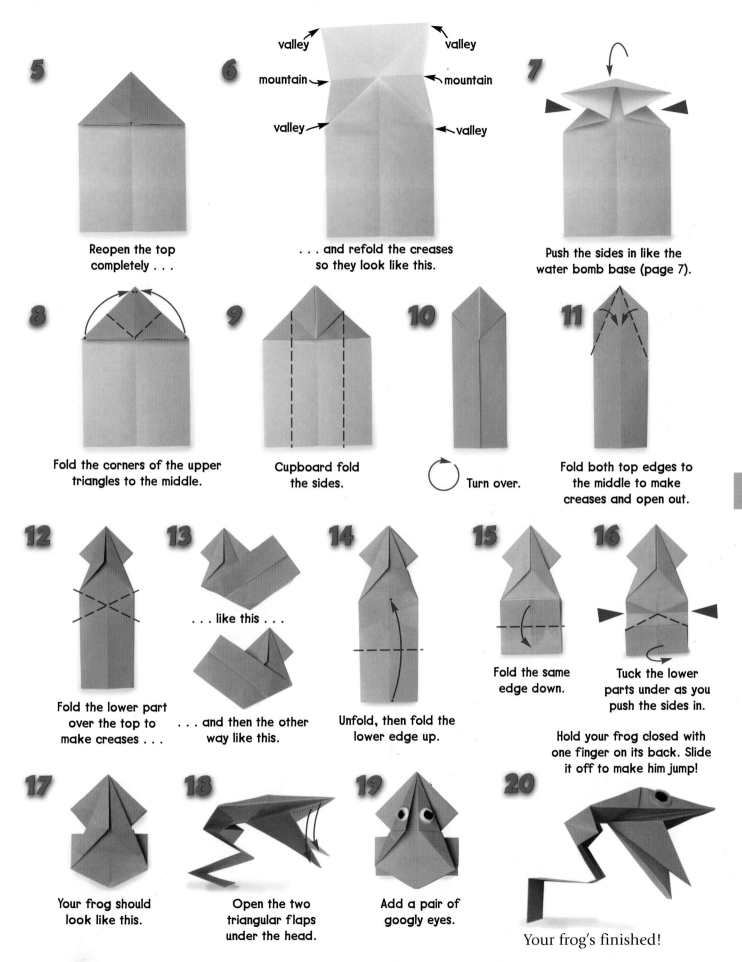

5 Reopen the top completely . . .

6 valley · valley · mountain · mountain · valley · valley
. . . and refold the creases so they look like this.

7 Push the sides in like the water bomb base (page 7).

8 Fold the corners of the upper triangles to the middle.

9 Cupboard fold the sides.

10 Turn over.

11 Fold both top edges to the middle to make creases and open out.

12 Fold the lower part over the top to make creases . . .

13 . . . like this . . .
. . . and then the other way like this.

14 Unfold, then fold the lower edge up.

15 Fold the same edge down.

16 Tuck the lower parts under as you push the sides in.

Hold your frog closed with one finger on its back. Slide it off to make him jump!

17 Your frog should look like this.

18 Open the two triangular flaps under the head.

19 Add a pair of googly eyes.

20 Your frog's finished!

School of Fish

You can make a school of these colorful fish in no time!

15 MINUTES

Start with an opened-up water bomb base (see page 7).

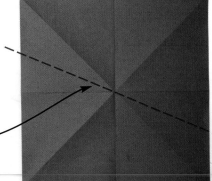

1

Make a fold that goes through the center of the paper.

2

These diagonal folds should align.

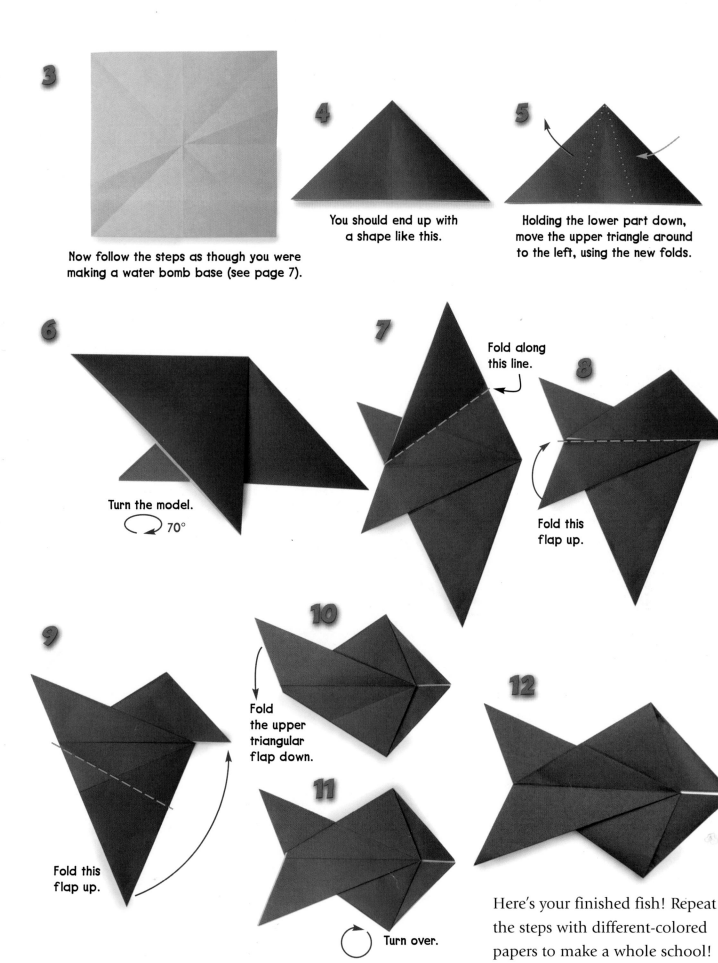

3

Now follow the steps as though you were making a water bomb base (see page 7).

4

You should end up with a shape like this.

5

Holding the lower part down, move the upper triangle around to the left, using the new folds.

6

Turn the model.
70°

7

Fold along this line.

8

Fold this flap up.

9

Fold this flap up.

10

Fold the upper triangular flap down.

11

Turn over.

12

Here's your finished fish! Repeat the steps with different-colored papers to make a whole school!

Duck

This looks just like a duck, but don't get it wet!

20 MINUTES

16

This duck is easier than it looks. The head's the key. Good luck!

1

pinch mark

Make one diagonal crease, then fold the other diagonal, making a pinch mark in the middle. Then fold it into a kite base (see page 6).

2

Fold the lower part up and crease along the dotted line.

The long edge should touch this point.

3

Make the crease only as far as here, then open it out.

4

Make a similar crease on the other side and open it out again.

5

Turn the model over and reverse the marked folds.

6

Push the sides together, and lay the model on its side.

7

Make a crease here. Then make an outside reverse fold (see page 6).

8

Make three more creases.

Make them into these folds.

9

inside reverse fold

outside reverse fold

mountain fold

10

Lift up the lower section and fold along this line.

11

Turn the model over and fold the similar section on the other side.

12

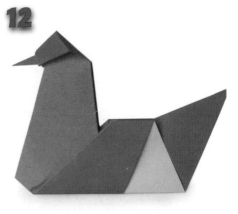

One duck is finished!

Windmill

You can make this windmill spin just by blowing on it!

30 MINUTES

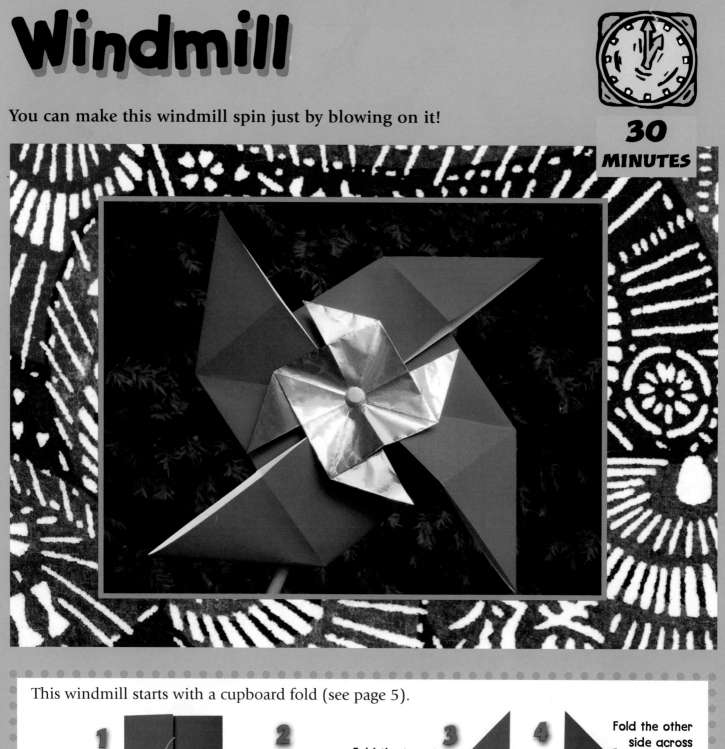

18

This windmill starts with a cupboard fold (see page 5).

1

The colored side should be outside.

2

Valley fold in half, then open again.

3

Fold the top across to meet the side, then open.

4

Fold the other side across in the same way, then open.

5

Fold the top down to meet the center crease you made first.

6

Fold the bottom to the middle, then open the last two folds.

7

Fold diagonally across the middle, like this.

8

Open the last fold, then fold in the opposite direction, like this.

9

Open the top part in the direction of the arrows.

10

Open it out and down.

11

Flatten the top like this, then fold the lower part in the same way.

12

Fold up this triangle.

13

Fold up the triangle on the opposite side.

14

You should have this shape.

15

Make another windmill from a square with sides half the size of this one.

Get an adult to help you fix your windmill to a stick with a thumbtack, and it's finished!

Dinosaur

From the age of the dinosaurs comes the huge seismosaurus!

Start with a kite base (see page 6).

1

Fold a kite base with the color on the inside.

2

Turn it over and fold the sides to the center.

3

Bring the flaps at the back around to the front.

4

Fold the corners down.

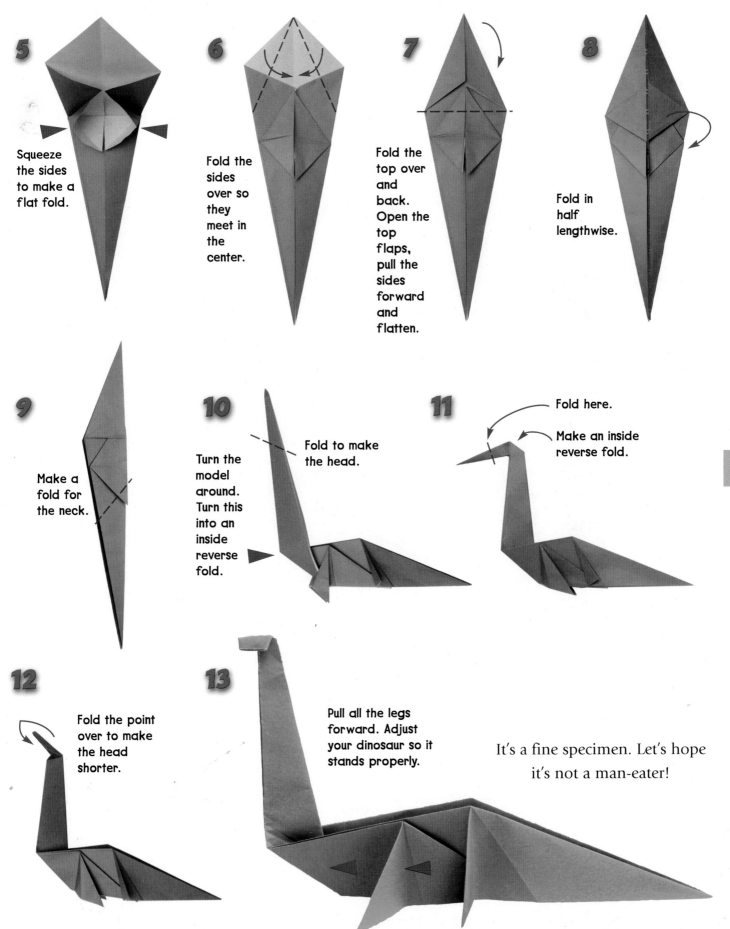

5 Squeeze the sides to make a flat fold.

6 Fold the sides over so they meet in the center.

7 Fold the top over and back. Open the top flaps, pull the sides forward and flatten.

8 Fold in half lengthwise.

9 Make a fold for the neck.

10 Turn the model around. Turn this into an inside reverse fold.

Fold to make the head.

11 Fold here.

Make an inside reverse fold.

12 Fold the point over to make the head shorter.

13 Pull all the legs forward. Adjust your dinosaur so it stands properly.

It's a fine specimen. Let's hope it's not a man-eater!

You can enjoy these paper flowers all year.

Start with a square base (see page 6).

1

Lift up the upper flap on the left to turn on the center line.

2

Open the flap and squash it down so the edge becomes the center.

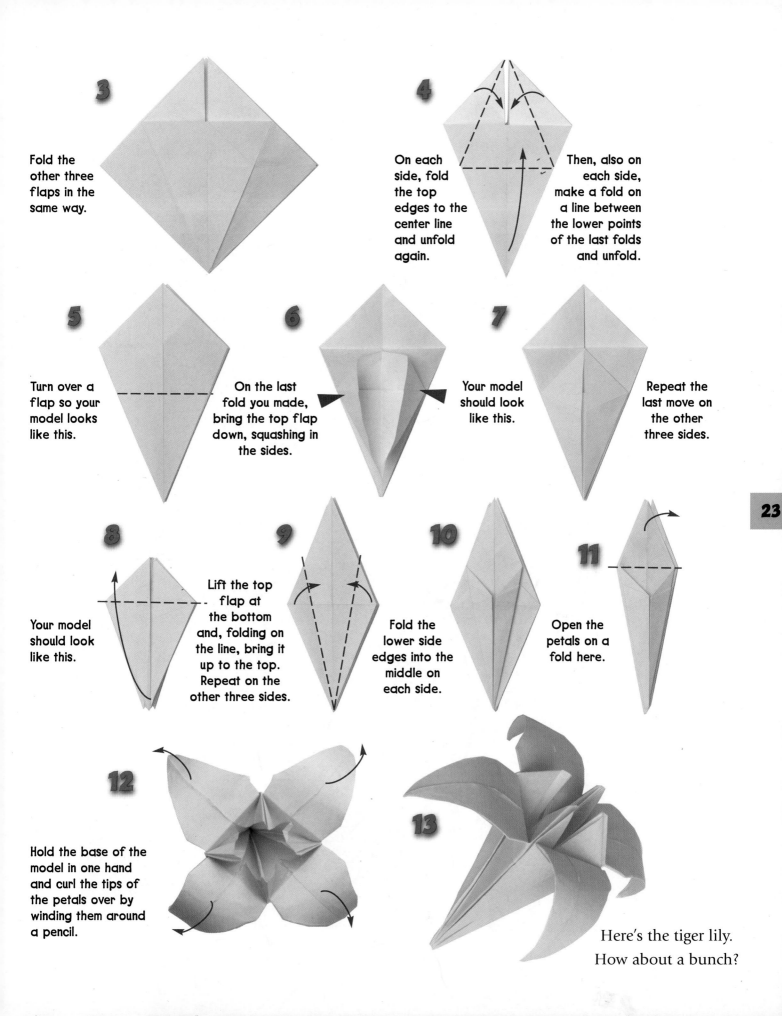

3

Fold the other three flaps in the same way.

4

On each side, fold the top edges to the center line and unfold again.

Then, also on each side, make a fold on a line between the lower points of the last folds and unfold.

5

Turn over a flap so your model looks like this.

6

On the last fold you made, bring the top flap down, squashing in the sides.

7

Your model should look like this.

Repeat the last move on the other three sides.

8

Your model should look like this.

9

Lift the top flap at the bottom and, folding on the line, bring it up to the top. Repeat on the other three sides.

10

Fold the lower side edges into the middle on each side.

11

Open the petals on a fold here.

23

12

Hold the base of the model in one hand and curl the tips of the petals over by winding them around a pencil.

13

Here's the tiger lily. How about a bunch?

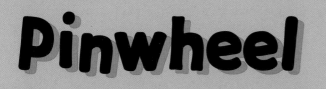

Pinwheel

This wheel looks like a puzzle, but it's not as hard as it seems!

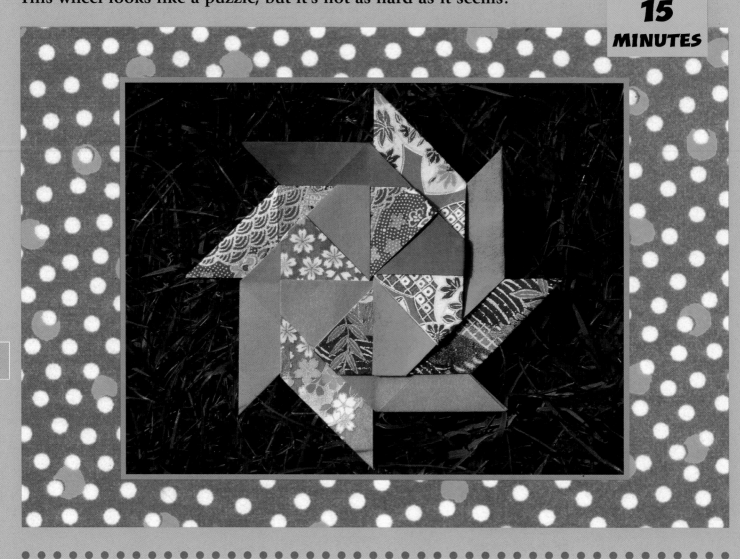

24

There are eight parts in this model, all folded in the same way.

1

Make two diagonal folds in your square.

2

Fold the top corners to the middle.

Mountain fold your model on the center line.

3

Fold both layers at the bottom diagonally.

4

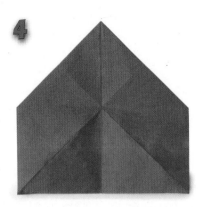

Open out the model like this.

5

Reverse the fold at the bottom, push it in, and lay it flat.

6

The result should look like this.

Here's another.

7

The second piece goes in the first piece like this.

8

Wrap the tip of the first piece around the second piece and tuck it in. Repeat on both sides.

9

Continue with more pieces.

10

One more piece will finish it.

11

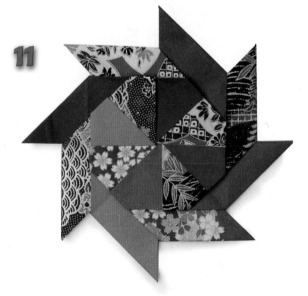

One pinwheel is finished!

Butterfly

Bring the garden indoors with this clever piece of folding.

26

Fold a water bomb base with the color on the outside (see page 7).

1

Fold the top down to touch the bottom edge.

2

Make a valley fold here.

Make mountain folds here.

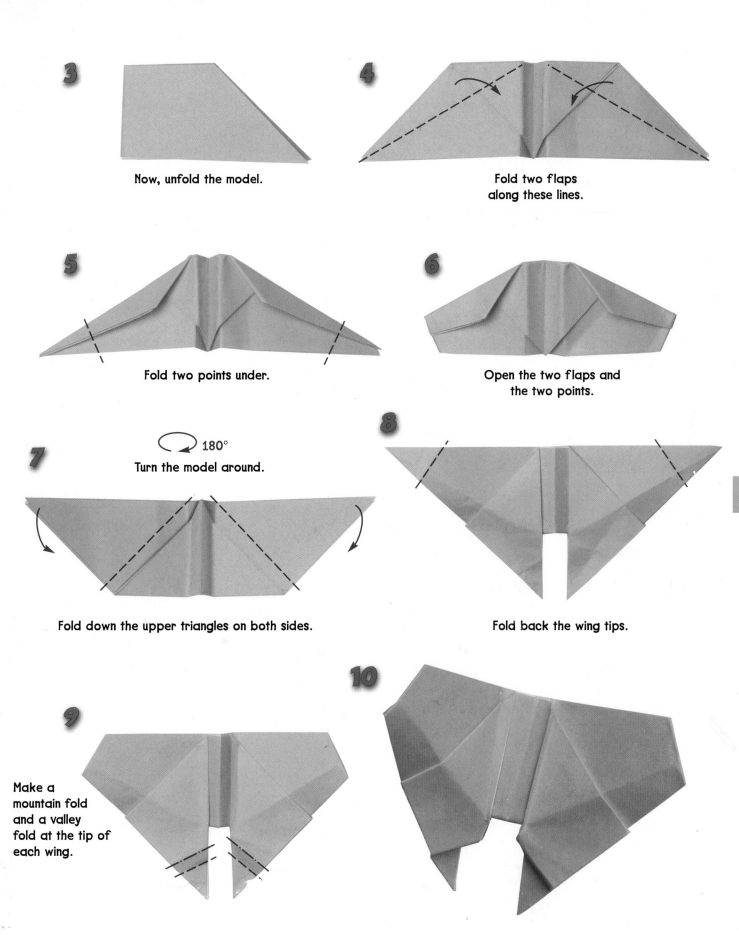

3

Now, unfold the model.

4

Fold two flaps along these lines.

5

Fold two points under.

6

Open the two flaps and the two points.

7

↻ 180°
Turn the model around.

Fold down the upper triangles on both sides.

8

Fold back the wing tips.

9

Make a mountain fold and a valley fold at the tip of each wing.

10

You've made a butterfly. Now make some more!

Flapping Crane

In Japan, origami cranes are believed to bring people good luck.

28

Start with a square base (see page 6). The open end should point down.

1

Fold the top triangular flaps into the center.

2

Make a fold with the top triangle, then open all three folds.

3

Open the point at the bottom of the square.

4

Flatten the new fold and turn the model over.

5

Repeat the fold on this side.

6

Fold the lower sides into the center.

7

Repeat on the other sides till the model looks like this.

8

Fold the lower parts at these lines and unfold.

9

Reverse inside fold to make the head.

Inside reverse fold the two lower parts (see page 5).

Pull down the wings.

10

To make the wings flap, hold the base of the neck and pull the tail. Gently!

You've finished the flapping crane. It's a classic origami model!

Water Bomb

It's fun to make, but use it outside unless you want to have to clean up!

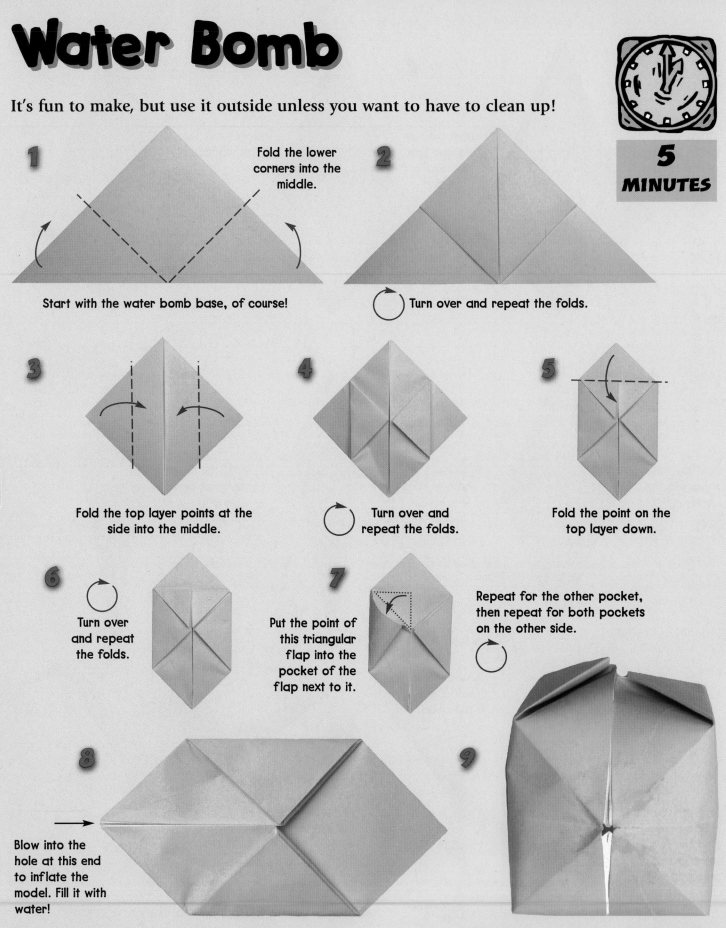

1 Fold the lower corners into the middle.

Start with the water bomb base, of course!

2 Turn over and repeat the folds.

3 Fold the top layer points at the side into the middle.

4 Turn over and repeat the folds.

5 Fold the point on the top layer down.

6 Turn over and repeat the folds.

7 Put the point of this triangular flap into the pocket of the flap next to it.

Repeat for the other pocket, then repeat for both pockets on the other side.

8 Blow into the hole at this end to inflate the model. Fill it with water!

9

Here is the water bomb. The rest is up to you!

Glossary

base   (BAYS) A combination of folds that can be used as a starting point for creating an origami model.

bird base   (BURD BAYS) A classic base formed by petal folding both sides of a square base.

contest   (KON-test) A game in which two or more people try to win.

crease   (KREES) A line formed by folding paper.

designs   (dih-ZYNZ) Decorative patterns.

divided   (dih-VYD-ed) Broken apart or separated.

fold   (FOHLD) To bring two parts of a sheet of paper together, usually flattening the paper.

googly eyes   (GOO-glee EYEZ) Plastic stick-on eyes with moving parts, used for making toys.

instructions   (in-STRUK-shunz) Explanations or directions.

mountain fold   (MOWN-tun FOHLD) A crease formed by folding paper out, up, and away from you.

origami   (awr-uh-GAH-mee) A Japanese word meaning "folding paper."

petal fold   (PEH-tul FOHLD) A fold in which a layer is lifted up and the sides are narrowed to form a point.

reverse fold   (rih-VERS FOHLD) A fold in which part of a flap is folded inside or outside another flap.

rotate   (ROH-tayt) To move in a circle.

square base   (SKWER BAYS) A simple base that uses just four creases.

squash   (SKWAHSH) A method in which a flap is separated and flattened.

symbols   (SIM-bulz) Objects or pictures that stand for something else.

valley fold   (VA-lee FOHLD) A crease made by folding paper in, down, and toward you.

waterbomb base   (WAW-ter BOM BAYS) A simple base that uses the square base creases.

Index

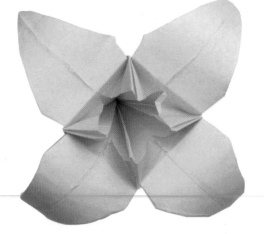

Web Sites

Due to the changing nature of Internet links, PowerKids Press has developed an online list of Web sites related to the subject of this book. This site is updated regularly. Please use this link to access the list:
www.powerkidslinks.com/myoa/origami/